CHINESE KNOTS *for* BEADED JEWELLERY

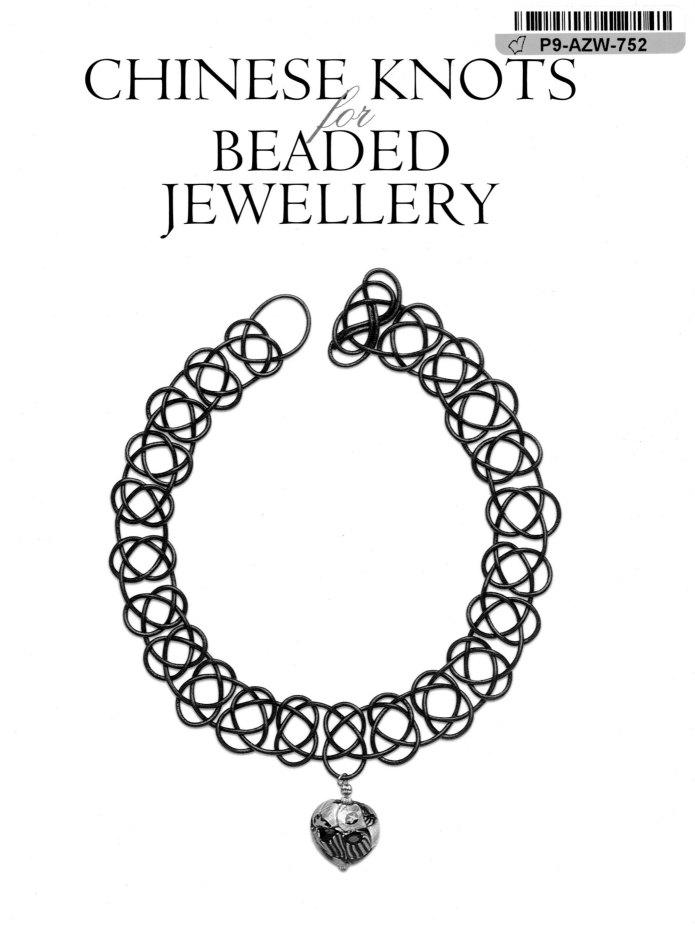

CHINESE KNOTS
for
BEADED JEWELLERY

Suzen Millodot

SEARCH PRESS

First published in Great Britain 2003

Search Press Limited
Wellwood, North Farm Road,
Tunbridge Wells, Kent TN2 3DR

Reprinted 2003 (twice), 2004, 2005

ISBN 0 85532 968 8

The Publishers and author can accept no responsibility for any
consequences arising from the information, advice or instructions
given in this publication.

Readers are permitted to reproduce any of the items in this book
for their personal use, or for the purposes of selling for charity, free
of charge and without the prior permission of the Publishers. Any
use of the items for commercial purposes is not permitted without
the prior permission of the Publishers.

Suppliers

If you have difficulty in obtaining any of the materials and
equipment mentioned in this book, then please visit the
Search Press website for details of suppliers:
www.searchpress.com

You are also invited to visit the author's website:
www.chineseknots.com

Alternatively, you can write to the Publishers at the address
above, for a current list of stockists, including firms who
operate a mail-order service.

Publisher's note

All the step-by-step photographs in this book feature the
author, Suzen Millodot, demonstrating how to tie Chinese
knots and how to make jewellery using Chinese knots.
No models have been used.

*I would like to thank Dianna Hui, in Hong Kong, who
taught me how to tie my first Chinese knots; Doreen and
Miriam of Dervish, who showed such interest and
encouraged me; my husband, Michel, who inspired me to
write this book and gave me constant support; and John
Dalton, my editor, who went through everything so
thoroughly and tied all the knots himself.*

Printed in Malaysia by Times Offset (M) Sdn Bhd

CONTENTS

INTRODUCTION

My husband and I went to live in Hong Kong in 1990, and it proved to be a fascinating experience. This book is about knotting, so I can only mention in passing the wonderful restaurants, the harbour, the skyline, the Star Ferry . . . the list could go on and on! Yu Hwa, a Chinese department store, was overwhelming, with wonderful silks, porcelain, paintings, rosewood furniture, beautiful jewellery with semiprecious stones, Chinese herbal medicines and exotic food – a trip up the escalator, from the basement to the top floor, was a feast for the eyes! But my favourite place was the Jade Market in Kowloon, an unprepossessing market full of little stalls under canvas awnings, unbearably hot in Hong Kong's humid summers, but so interesting that one almost forgot the discomfort in the excitement of the place! They sold jade items (beads, pendants, necklaces and bracelets), silver and gold jewellery and an abundance of other beautiful items. One had to bargain for a good deal, and a rule of thumb (for people who are not expert on precious stones) was not to believe anyone and not to spend a large sum of money for any item.

It was at this market that I was introduced to Chinese knots. I found a stall holder sitting next to her table effortlessly knotting cord with beads. She only had enough English to tell me the price and to assure me that the beads were real jade, real amber, etc., and she certainly did not expect to show me how she did the knots!

Where was I to learn? None of my friends or acquaintances knew how to do them, and I could not find any courses or lessons, certainly not in English. I finally came across a beautiful book written in English, but the instructions were too complicated for me (then an utter novice) to learn the basics. Although I managed to tie some of the knots, I could not work out how to get them in the correct place, or how to finish a necklace. So I resigned myself to remaining mystified!

Several years later we moved to another neighbourhood and, while out shopping, I found a little shop, tucked away behind the supermarket, that sold necklaces with beads and pendants. I started chatting with the owner, whose English was very good, and one day I asked her if she could teach me how to tie Chinese knots. 'Yes', she said, 'there are details of the lessons on that notice in the window'. Of course, you have guessed it, the notice was all in Chinese! Anyway, I took a series of lessons and learned all about the famous button knot – the various ways of tying it, how to move its position on the cord and how to combine it with other knots. From then on I was hooked and I started searching for beads with large holes, and knotting necklaces with pendants and Chinese coins. The adventure had begun!

Amber pendant necklace with a prosperity knot tied with black and rust-brown cord (see page 50).

Chinese knots are usually tied with a beautiful silky cord known by the unglamorous name of rattail! This cord is very decorative in itself and a single Chinese knot tied with it can be large, showy and complete in itself. Add a few more knots and some beads and you have an original necklace that is much stronger than a silver or gold chain. As well as being unique and valuable, your knotted necklaces can be as elegant or extravagant, and as understated or overstated as you want them to be!

Although the art of Chinese knotting includes many intricately combined knots, only the basic knots shown on pages 18–20 are really suitable for knotted jewellery.

To my mind, the simplicity of one beautiful knot is enough; it can satisfy our souls in a way that something more complex cannot. I think that one simple knot, or a series of knots and beads is incredibly elegant, and being able to create it yourself is a wonderful antidote to our fast-paced high-tech lives!

The most frequently used knot is the button knot. Most people have seen this knot at some time or another as little buttons on traditional Chinese dresses and jackets. On first seeing it, one wants to examine it more carefully and to meditate over its seemingly endless weaving in and out of itself in a perfect ball. In Chinese tradition this endless pattern is considered a symbol of good luck – the wearer's longevity and nobility will continue forever with great vitality! It is a graphic representation of the cyclical nature of all existence in Chinese Buddhism.

In this book, I try to demystify this interesting little knot and to show you how it can be used in various ways to make unique, elegant, handmade necklaces, bracelets and earrings.

This decorative knot can also be very functional. Pairs of button knots can be made to slide along the cord allowing a necklace to be lengthened or shortened at will. This method of closure eliminates the need for special findings to finish a necklace, and the same necklace can be a choker or a long necklace.

The button knot, with all its variations, is my favourite knot and, as such, I make no apology for the fact that it features in a number of the projects in this book. There are, however, lots of projects tied with other knots which I hope you will enjoy. When you have practised tying the knots and become more confident and adventurous, I am sure you will soon start to work up your own designs.

Opposite
From left to right:
An earring featuring a Pan Chang knot, beads (one of which is covered with a matching material) and a tassel.
Turquoise pendant necklace, featuring double button knots and Thai silver beads.
An earring embellished with a plafond knot and a button knot.

History

Chinese knotting (and other Chinese folk crafts) came perilously close to being entirely lost during the last century. Traditionally, Chinese women handed down craft lore from generation to generation, but, as it was never recorded as written instructions, it all but disappeared. Relics could be found in Chinese museums, but they were usually labelled as 'a tradition that we used to have'.

It is difficult to say when ornamental knotting started in China. Fabrics and cords are not as durable as the materials used in other arts and crafts, so early examples of Chinese knots have long turned to dust. Knotted rope belts, however, are known to have existed as long ago as 1122BCE (the Chou Dynasty). Pictures from the Han dynasty (200BCE–220CE) show knots and bows on waist sashes; recently, decorative loops and knots have been found in tombs from that era. From 618 to 906CE knotting was beginning to be used to adorn other works of art, but the height of its popularity came during the Ching Dynasty (1644 to 1911CE), when knots adorned clothes, jewellery, furniture and other belongings of all classes, from rich to poor.

At the beginning of last century, the pastime of knotting was widespread and, especially on festivals and at weddings, beautiful knotwork created by the participants could be seen everywhere. The designs of the knots were fashioned after the symbols of happiness, longevity, Buddhist treasures and prosperity, etc. Sadly these skills disappeared within two generations.

In the mid 1970's, however, with the increasing prosperity of Taiwan, several young Chinese artists, most notably Lydia Chen and Nelson T.J. Chang, realised the importance of preserving this dying art form. At the same time, Wang Chen-Kai, a master knotter from China, began working at the National Palace Museum in Taipei. The Echo Publishing Company of Taipei succeeded in finding a few of the remaining 'keepers' of the knotting tradition. With trembling hands, these elderly people showed the youngsters how to tie the knots. After much dedicated research and lots of practice these young people revived the craft, taught it to others, recorded instructions and published books. The interest they generated was beyond their wildest expectations. In Taipei, Nelson Chang opened a large store selling knotted products. The store also contains a museum with a stunning exhibition of complex knotted works. Nowadays, there are classes in schools and colleges, and also television programmes about knotting. Thus, in the nick of time, the art of knotting, along with other Chinese folk crafts, was saved.

Traditional Chinese hanging featuring, from top to bottom: double connection knot; clover leaf knot; double button knots; large Pan Chang knot, known as a reunion knot; a lion dog to frighten away evil spirits; and many fire cracker knots, also to frighten evil spirits.

About knots

Knots can be functional or decorative. In days gone by, when great sailing ships plied the seas, knots were entirely functional, and were developed by sailors to tie ropes to solid objects such as poles or ring bolts. These knots have practical names such as *Half Hitch*, *Clove Hitch* and *Reef Knot*.

Many of you will be familiar with the craft of macramé which involves knotting cord and string to form plant pot holders, wall hangings and bags. These decorative knots are basically the same as the functional knots, but the names have changed: the functional *Cow Hitch* becomes a decorative *Lark's Head Knot*; the *Carrick Bend* becomes the *Josephine Knot*; and a variation of the *Reef Knot* twists around to become macramé's decorative *Granny Knot*.

Traditional Chinese knots, however, were developed purely for decoration. They include loops and swirls to form intricate and symbolic designs drawn from nature, folk tales and the Chinese language. The semi-stiff cord used for tying Chinese knots holds the shape of curves and loops (eliminating the need for other anchoring knots),

so a Chinese knot can be quite self-contained and expressive on its own. Some Chinese knots are the same as nautical and macramé knots but, of course, they have completely different names! Macramé's *Josephine Knot*, for example, becomes the Chinese *Double Coin Knot*, and the sailors' *Turks Head Knot* (a stopper or terminal knot) becomes the Chinese *Button Knot*, variations of which allow it to be tied as an intermediate knot in the middle of the cord.

One interesting fact about all the knots in the various traditions is that they are all combinations of two very simple knots: the *Half Hitch* (or *loop*); and the *Overhand Knot*, which is a half hitch through which one end is tucked.

The well-known reef knot, for example, consists of two overhand knots; one tied left over right, the other right over left. When you tie shoelaces, you will most probably tie a *Reef Bow* which is a reef knot with the ends doubled and looped into each other on the second overhand knot. If you can tie these knots you have the ability to learn any basic knot!

The Chinese devised patterns that combined several different types of simple knots to form complex and beautiful representational art, often depicting birds, butterflies and other auspicious designs. Beautiful as they are, these intricate knots do not lend themselves readily to making necklaces, so they are beyond the scope of this book.

MATERIALS AND EQUIPMENT

Cords

Many types of cord can be used to tie Chinese knots: cotton, silk, hemp, string, leather, synthetics – in fact, you could use anything that can be tied. Look in craft shops, sewing supply shops, upholstery and curtain material suppliers, or even fishing tackle and camping gear outlets.

The best cord for the beginner is single colour, smooth, round, fairly thick cord that is semi-stiff.

Single colour cords show off the design of the knot, especially when a knot is worked with two or more different colours. The pattern in variegated cords will create confusion. Similarly, a smooth cord is better than a textured cord, as any texture will spoil the essential neatness that is characteristic of Chinese knot designs.

You can work with flat or square cords, but I suggest that you leave these shapes until you have mastered tying the knots with round cord.

Choose a fairly thick cord so that your efforts will be visible. I once used embroidery thread to make a lovely button knot but I needed a magnifying glass to see it!

The most important characteristic of a cord, however, is its degree of firmness. The ideal cord is semi-firm – not too rigid, nor too pliable. Rigid cords will not take on the shape you need, they are hard to control and uncomfortable for the fingers. On the other hand, a really pliable cord will not take on any shape at all! When choosing a cord, make a loop and see if the cord holds the shape; if it does not flop or try to straighten itself out, it will be suitable. An elastic or stretchy cord is not good as it can slip out of shape easily.

Synthetic cord is useful as the ends can be lightly burned to seal them and stop them from slipping. They do not fray easily.

Most of the projects are worked with a 2mm thick, satin cord (called rattail), which is available in lots of colours. I also use a firmer, braided cotton cord for some knots.

Beads, pendants and findings

The world of beads is very exciting and addictive, so be warned! Beads can be made out of almost anything; clay, glass, metal, plastic, wood, polymer clay, ceramic and semiprecious stones. There are many good books about beads, describing the merits of each material, so I will not attempt to go into a lot of detail here. Apart from selecting beads that look nice and complement your knots, there is only one important question to consider: is the hole large enough for the cord to pass through?

On several occasions, I have found some beautiful beads, bought them and then found that they were impossible to use. Now, when I go out searching for beads and pendants, I always take short lengths of the cords I intend to use.

The holes in some types of beads are not consistent. You may find it easy to pass the cord through one, but not through others, so check all the beads you buy. The holes in some beads, especially those made from soft materials, can be smoothed and enlarged using a small, round, pointed file. Unfortunately, most of the beads with problem holes are made from hard materials such as semiprecious stones, which need specialist drills and equipment to enlarge them.

Do not be tempted into buying cheap beads. They will always look cheap, and your handiwork is worth more than that! Several times I have seen intricately knotted necklaces (that must have taken hours to work) decorated with beads that few people would want to wear. What a waste of all that work!

Findings are used on some of the necklaces. Again, there are lots to choose from, but I find that chunky closures complement my designs more than dainty ones, which can also be difficult to use.

For the projects in this book, I list the sizes and shapes of the beads and pendants I used, but, as it is virtually impossible to duplicate them, it will be up to you to choose your own.

Other items

Apart from cords, beads and pendants, there are a few items that will prove helpful additions to your work box.

Scissors Neat, pointed cord ends are important for threading, so sharp scissors are a must (blunt ones are useless and spoil the cord without cutting it).

PVA glue Applying this to cord ends is by far the best way to prepare them for threading through beads. Knots with large loops can be stiffened with diluted PVA (mixed ten parts water to one part glue).

Paint brush This is used to apply PVA glue to the cord; any cheap brush will do.

Sticky tape Clear adhesive tape or masking tape can also be used to prepare the cord ends.

Lighter A small disposable cigarette lighter is ideal for flame-sealing the cut ends of cords.

Cork mat Although it is possible to tie Chinese knots in your hand, many of them are best laid out on a flat surface, especially when you are learning how to tie them. 1cm (½in) thick cork is the ideal material; a cork wall tile will make a good working surface. Cork place mats (for protecting tables from hot dishes) could also be used, but these need to be at least 20cm (8in) diameter. If you are eager to start and cannot find a suitable piece of cork, a sheet of corrugated cardboard with a smooth surface will work well.

Pins I like to use dressmaker's pins to anchor the cord on the cork mat while I am tying the knots. They are fine enough not damage the cord. Those with small coloured balls on the head are the easiest to handle.

Tweezers Fine-pointed tweezers, with smooth gripping surfaces, can prove helpful when weaving the cord through cramped spaces. They must be used very gently, however, as they can make unsightly indentations on the cord.

Instant glue This is useful for fastening beads that are not held in place by knots, and for sticking the cut ends of cord to the underside of some knots, especially those tied with leather.

File A small, round pointed file can be used to smooth and enlarge the holes in some beads.

Needles Some of the flatter knots are not very stable when tied with silky cords, so a few stitches sewn through the back of the knot will help retain its shape. A large-eyed tapestry needle is useful for threading cord back through knots at the ends of necklaces and bracelets.

Pliers Flat-nosed pliers, with short, fine, round points are used to fix metal findings on to the ends of necklaces and bracelets, to open and close jump rings, and to bend head pins.

Wire cutters These are needed to cut head pins and other wire findings.

My work surface consists of a beanbag tray on which I have stuck pieces of cork tiles.

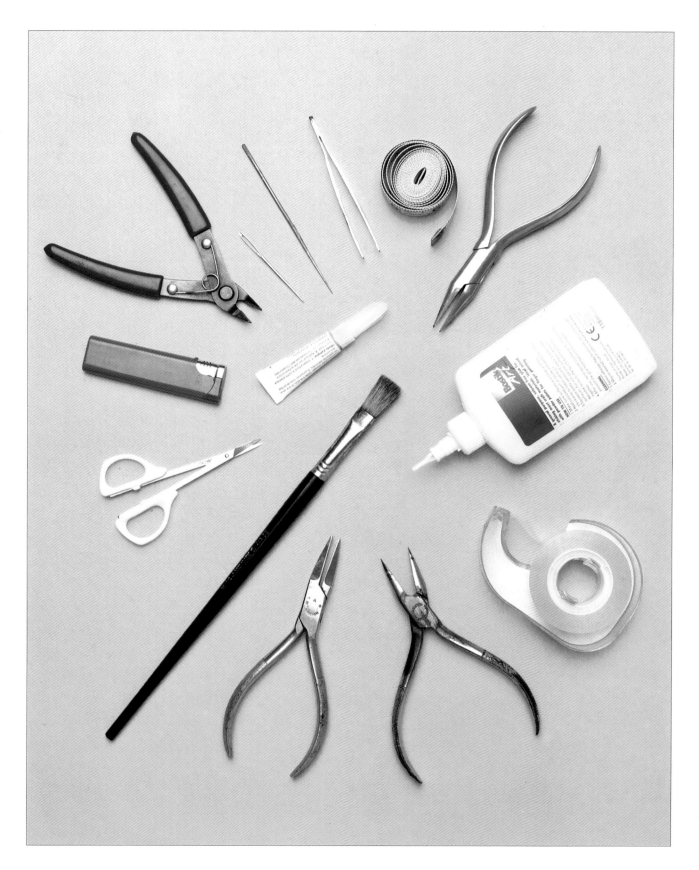

PREPARING CORDS

Before embarking on any project you have to decide on the length of cord you need. Always err on the long side, as it is very upsetting to be almost finished only to find that you do not have enough cord. Cord tends to fray when cut, making it difficult to tie some knots, so I always stiffen the ends using one of the techniques shown opposite.

Calculating lengths of cord

The total length of cord required depends on the final length of the necklace (or bracelet) and the type and number of knots in the design. Although I have included the required lengths of cord for the project necklaces, you may want to design your own pieces, so here are a few notes about calculating the length of cord you will need.

Necklace lengths

The following table lists the average length of different types of necklace.

Choker	40cm	(16in)
Necklace with fastener	45cm	(18in)
Necklace without fastener*	70cm	(28in)

This measurement will comfortably go over the head. It should be used as the maximum length for necklaces tied with sliding knots which can then be shortened by sliding the knots apart.

You can make this type of necklace longer if you wish, but you should allow at least 30cm (12in) of cord after the last stationary knot on each side of the necklace, to enable the sliding knots to be tied.

Cord lengths for knots

The following table shows the approximate length of 2mm cord required to tie single knots.

Button knot	8.5cm	(3½in)
Sliding button knot	9.5cm	(3¾in)
Double button knot	25cm	(10in)
Prosperity knot	40cm	(16in)

The following table shows how to determine the total length of 2mm cord required to make an 80cm (32in) necklace with one double button knot, ten single button knots and two sliding button knots.

Length of necklace	80cm	(32in)
Double button knot	25cm	(10in)
Ten button knots	85cm	(35in)
Two sliding knots	19cm	(7½in)
Allowance for tying the sliding knots	60cm	(24in)
Total length	269cm	(108½in)

It is better to have too much than too little, so I would add a small allowance for possible additions and cut a 300cm (120in) length of cord.

Note that, to allow for all the knots, you have to start with a much longer cord than you might have imagined!

Cutting and sealing cord ends

Cut cord ends will invariably start to fray, making it difficult to thread the cord through beads and knots. This problem can be overcome by sealing the ends with PVA glue, sticky tape or a flame. Cut the cord on the diagonal rather than straight across; the tapered ends make sealing and threading easier.

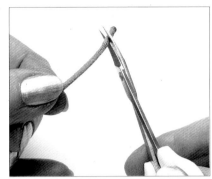

Always cut cord ends on the diagonal.

Sealed cord ends, from the left: PVA glue; sticky tape; and flame sealed.

PVA glue

If the holes in the beads are uneven, then the cord ends must be very stiff, and PVA glue is the sealing method to choose. It may be annoying to wait while the glue dries, but it is well worth the effort and can save spending hours trying to get the cord through a stubborn bead!

Sticky tape

You can also create suitable points on the ends of cords by wrapping them with sticky tape. The tape will make the cord ends slightly larger, so this method is not suitable for beads with holes that are only just big enough to take the diameter of the cord.

Flame sealing

For projects that do not include beads between the knots, it is only necessary to seal the last 3mm ($\frac{1}{8}$in) of each cord end. An easy way of sealing the ends of most man-made fibre cords is with a flame. The small flame produced by a cigarette lighter is more than sufficient.

Use a small paint brush to apply the PVA glue to the cord. Use as much glue as the cord will absorb, all around, and up to 2.5cm (1in) from each end of the cord. Support the wet ends so they are not touching anything, then leave them to dry for at least an hour (longer for slow-drying glues) until the ends are very hard. Now cut the ends again to make sharp, needle-like points.

Place the corner of a short length of sticky tape under the cord . . .

. . . then roll it round the cord with your finger and thumb.

Place the end of the cord into the flame (rather than apply the flame to the cord) for a fraction of a second. If you apply the flame for any longer, the end of the cord will become an ugly brown knob. I also use this method to seal any trimmed ends that are left when the knotting is finished.

GALLERY OF BASIC KNOTS

The knots shown here and on the following pages are used for the projects in this book, on their own or in combination with others.

Button Knot
tied with one end of the cord
(see pages 22–23)

The variation below has had the top loop pulled into the knot.

Button Knots
tied with both ends of the cord
(see pages 28–29)

Double Button Knot
tied with one cord
(see page 34)

Double Button Knot
tied with two cords
(see page 32)

Button Knots
*each tied with one end of cord round
another coloured cord*
(see page 36)

Sliding Button Knots
*each tied with one end of a cord round the
other end. Always used in pairs to allow the
length of necklaces to be adjusted.*
(see page 24)

Flat Button Knot
(see pages 38–39)

Double Coin Knot
(see page 44)

Double Connection Knot
(see page 48)

Cross Knot
front (left) and back (right)
(see pages 40–41)

Clover Leaf Knot
(see page 52)

Good Luck Knot
(see page 56)

Virtue Knot
(see page 70)

Pan Chang Knot
(see pages 60–61

Round Brocade Knot
(see page 68)

Prosperity Knot
(see page 49)

Plafond Knot
(see pages 76–77)

Snake Knot
(see page 64)

Flat knot
(see page 74)

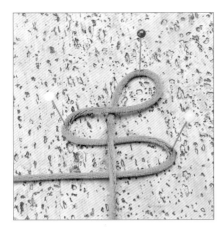

Pinning the cord to a cork mat helps maintain the shape of the knotting.

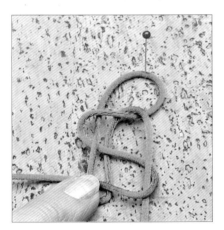

Removing some of the pins will become necessary to weave the cord over and under itself.

Tying knots

Before starting on a project, practise tying the knots using a 1m (1yd) length of cord. Some knots can be tied in the hand, but others are best planned out on a cork mat and temporarily held in place with pins while you work out where the end should go next – you will find it easier to follow the step-by step sequence without losing your place.

To help you even more, fix an enlarged copy of the knotting layout on the cork mat; you should have enough space to follow the instructions and maintain the correct proportions of the knot.

The shape of the knot is determined by the way the knotting is tightened. This is the most crucial part of Chinese knotting, and it can make or break your knot. It is most important to tighten a knot slowly and carefully, and to work each section of the cord as evenly and accurately as possible. Where necessary, I have included arrows on the diagrams to show you the directions in which to pull the cord.

Study the layout of each knot before you start, and make a mental note of the path of each part of the cord before you pull it tight. Always start tightening from the point where you began to tie the knot, methodically working out the slack, loop by loop, until you reach the end of the knot, repositioning the pins as necessary to retain the shape. If a kink develops, work it out by gently twisting the cord as you tighten.

The final form of the knot is determined by how tight you make the loops; this is your decision, but I suggest that loose knots with long loops are not practical for necklaces and bracelets. Knots with short even loops (or no visible loops at all) are more suitable, and they are better at keeping their shape.

Tighten the knot gently and slowly.

Working from the starting point, pull the cords through the knot to maintain the shape of the top loop.

The finished knot. Its final shape depends on the tightness of the cords.

BUTTON KNOT

This is my favourite knot, and I hardly ever make a necklace without using at least one of them. It is very attractive, with the cord weaving in and out of itself to form a ball. In Chinese tradition this seemingly endless pattern is considered a symbol of good luck, and it is a graphic representation of the cyclical nature of all existence in Chinese Buddhism.

   The button knot can be tied with one end of a single cord, it can be tied round a second cord to form a sliding button knot or a sequence of different coloured knots, and it can be tied with two ends of a cord to create a loop on one side of the knot. Other variations include a double button knot (see pages 32 and 34) and a flat button knot (see pages 38–39).

Button knot tied with one end of a cord.

Button knots tied with one end of a cord round another.

Button knot tied with both ends of a single cord.

Tying the knot with one end of a cord

Practise tying this knot with a 1m (1yd) length of cord. Start about 10cm (4in) from the left-hand end, and concentrate on getting all the unders and overs correctly aligned and creating a neat round knot. The position of the finished knot is not important at this stage as it can be moved quite easily (see page 25).

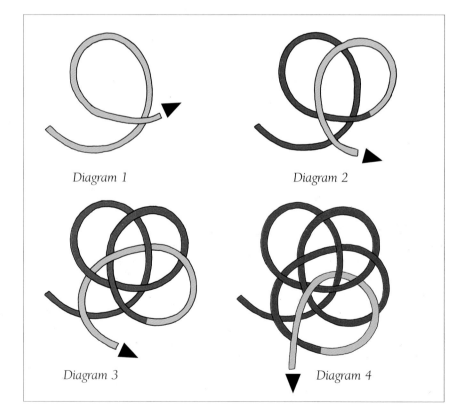

Diagram 1

Diagram 2

Diagram 3

Diagram 4

1. Hold the cord with your left thumb and forefinger, then make a loop (diagram 1).

2. Make a second loop, on top of and slightly overlapping the first one, to create three spaces (diagram 2).

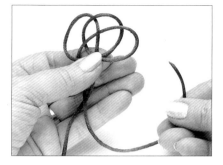

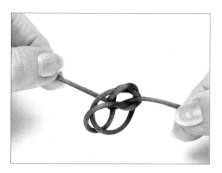

3. Take the cord down through the right-hand space, up through the centre, down through the left-hand space and round over the anchored end of the cord. Pull the cord through to create a new loop at the right-hand side (diagram 3).

4. Now take the cord down through the new right-hand space and back up through the centre loop to complete the knotting (diagram 4).

5. Check that all the overs and unders are correct (see diagram 4), then, working slowly and evenly, pull both ends of the cord to close the knot.

6. Continue pulling the knot closed; as the knot begins to take shape at least one of the loops will remain open.

7. Starting at the left-hand side, follow the path of the cord through the knot; note that you are continually rotating the top of the knot away from you. Working in this direction, close the open loop by gently pulling out the loop below.

8. Rotate the top of the knot away from you, then pull the cord to tighten the next loop.

Tightening tip
Always work round the knot in the same direction, holding the knot in one hand and tightening the loops with the other.

9. Tighten the last loop by pulling the right-hand end of the cord.

10. The completed knot. If parts of it are still slack, repeat steps 7–9.

Tying a sliding button knot

This knot is worked in the same way as that shown on pages 22–23, except it is tied around a second cord. A pair of knots can be used to close a necklace by adjusting its length. This method can also be used to tie different coloured knots side by side. You will need at least 30cm (12in) of cord for tying each knot, so practise tying them on each end of a 1m (1yd) length of cord.

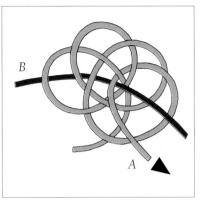

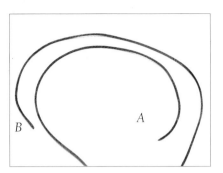

1. Begin by arranging the ends of the length of cord as shown.

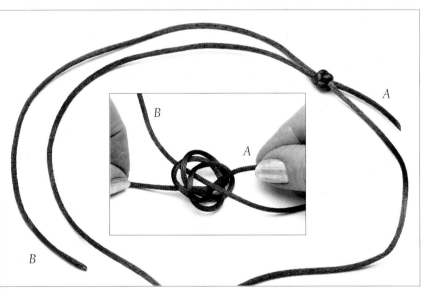

2. Referring to the instructions on pages 22–23 and the diagram above, use working end A to tie a loose button knot round cord B. Carefully tighten the knot as shown on page 23.

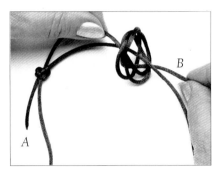

3. Turn the cord over, so that the first knot is at the left-hand side, then use the working end B to tie the second knot around cord A.

4. Pull the second knot tight, then test that the knots slide apart by pulling the cord ends A and B.

Knotting tip

When tying button knots round a holding cord, every time you take the cord upwards it should be behind the holding cord, every time you bring it downwards it should pass in front of the holding cord.

Button knot and bead necklace

This simple necklace is decorated with button knots and beads, and uses sliding button knots as the closure. The knotting must be symmetrical about the centre bead, so all the knots must be sized and spaced correctly. This involves moving the knots along the cord after they have been tied (see photographs and diagrams below).

This necklace has a maximum length of 62cm (24in). The sliding button knots allow it to be reduced to 40cm (16in).

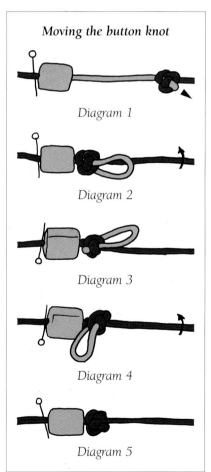

You will need

2.6m (102in) of 2mm satin cord
One large square bead
Six small flat washer beads
Two large decorative cylinder beads
Four flat medium-sized hexagonal or round washer beads
Two medium-sized round beads

1. Position a small washer bead, the large square bead and a second washer bead in the middle of the cord and anchor one side with a dressmaker's pin. Then, referring to pages 22–23, tie a button knot with the right-hand cord. The tightened knot will end up away from the bead and must be moved.

2. Rotate the knot to find the loop which links to the cord at the left-hand side (diagram 1).

3. Pull out this loop until the knot is up against the bead (diagram 2).

4. Rotate the knot again to find the loop that links to the bottom of the open loop (diagram 3), then pull this loop through the knot (diagram 4).

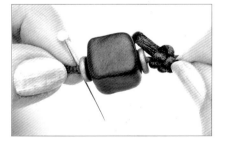

5. Continue rotating the knot and pulling the cord through it until you have pulled through eight loops (diagram 5).

Moving the button knot

Diagram 1

Diagram 2

Diagram 3

Diagram 4

Diagram 5

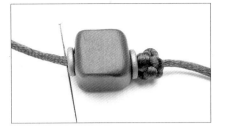

6. Close the last loop by pulling the right-hand end of the cord.

7. Tie and move another button knot up against the right-hand side of the beads. If necessary, tweak the shapes of one or both of the knots to equalise them.

Tightening tip

Finished knots on a necklace should be quite tight. If they are left too loose, they will tighten during wear and gaps may appear between them. However, you can always re-tighten the knots – it is never too late!

8. Now work up each side of the necklace, adding beads and knots. Check the positions of the knots at regular intervals to ensure that the sides of the necklace are symmetrical.

9. Trim off the ends of the cords to make the lengths equal, and to leave at least 30cm (12in) of cord from the last knots to allow for the sliding knots to be tied.

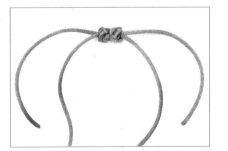

10. Referring to page 24, make a sliding knot on each side of the necklace, then move them so that they are equidistant from the end of each cord.

11. Trim the ends of the cords to leave 2–3mm (1/8in).

12. Seal the trimmed ends with a flame as shown on page 17.

Opposite
The finished necklace and two variations made with button knots and sliding button knots. The adjustable length afforded by the sliding knots make these necklaces versatile and comfortable to wear.

26

Tying button knots with two cord ends

Sometimes you may need to tie a knot with two cord ends; either with both ends of a single cord (to make a loop on one side of the knot), or with the ends of two different cords threaded through beads. Practise tying the knot using both ends of a 1m (1yd) length of cord.

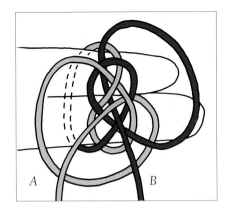

1. Place the middle of the cord behind your index finger and anchor cord end (A) with your little finger. Take cord end (B) round your thumb and back over itself. You now have two loops.

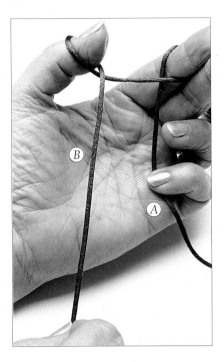

2. Lift the loop off your thumb . . .

3. . . . turn it over (as with a page of a book) and place it on top of the loop on your index finger. . .

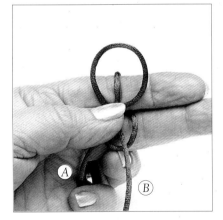

4. . . . then anchor the cords with your thumb.

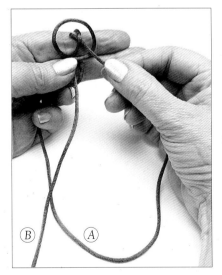

5. Check that cord A is under cord B, then thread the end of cord A through the loop on your index finger as shown.

6. Pull the end of the cord A upwards through the loops to make an open basket shape.

7. Bring cord end A down under cord B, then take it up through the middle of the basket shape.

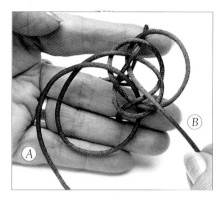

8. Pull cord A to leave a loop at the left-hand side of the basket shape. Take cord B round to the top of the basket, over the loop on the index finger and up through the centre of the basket shape to leave another loop on the right-hand side.

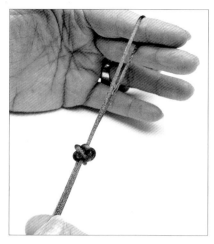

9. Check that all the overs and unders are correct (see diagram opposite), then pull both cords to close the knot.

Button knot and bead necklace

This necklace is made with two lengths of cord. When selecting the beads, ensure that you can thread both cords through their centres. If the holes are slightly too small, you may be able to use a fine, round file to open them up. The finished necklace is 43cm (17in) long. It is closed with a hook and ring fastener.

You will need

Two, 2.6m (102in) lengths of 2mm satin cord

One large round decorative bead

Four No. 10, four No. 8 and thirty No. 6 brass flat washers

Eight nickel shakeproof washers

Two medium and two small round glass beads

Two cylindrical glass beads

Hook and ring fastener

1. Centre the middle group of beads on both cords, then anchor one side with a dressmaker's pin.

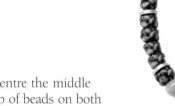

2. Place the group of beads behind your index finger and, referring to the instructions opposite, tie a button knot with both cords. Then, referring to page 25, move the button knot close to the beads. Note that, because the knot is tied with two cord ends, you have to tighten the loops in two separate groups of four.

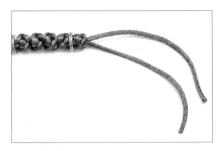

3. Remove the pin and make a knot on the other side of the centre set of beads.

4. Build up each side of the necklace with beads, washers and button knots until they have reached the required length.

5. Equalise the cords on each side of the necklace, trim each pair 7.5cm (3in) from the last knot, then lightly seal all ends with a flame.

6. At one end of the necklace, pass both cords through the fastener ring in opposite directions.

7. Thread the end of one cord on a large-eyed tapestry needle, then take the cord end back through the last two button knots.

8. Referring to step 7, take the other cord end back through just the last button knot. Trim off the excess lengths of cord and seal the ends with a flame. Repeat steps 6–8 for the hook end of the fastener.

Opposite
The finished project necklace and two other designs that were tied in a similar manner.

Double button knot necklace

Larger button knots can be made by tying them with two cords, either as shown in this project or by tying a knot with one cord then weaving that cord round through the knot again (see page 34). This necklace incorporates two double button knots as part of the centre pendant design and single button knots on each side. The finished necklace, which is fastened with sliding button knots, will be 88cm (34in) long.

You will need

260cm (102in) 2mm satin cord
Large circular pendant
Medium round decorative Thai silver bead
Two Thai decorated long bicone-shaped silver beads

1. Centre the large pendant on the cord, then, referring to pages 22–23, use the doubled cord to make a button knot.

2. Carefully pull the knot tight, ensuring that the two cords sit side by side right through the knot.

3. Referring to page 25, move the knot tight against the bead.

4. Thread a round bead on both lengths of cord, then repeat steps 1–3 to work another double knot against this bead.

5. Separate the cords, then make single button knots on each cord. Thread a long bead on each side, then secure in place with another button knot. Finally, equalise the remaining lengths of cord, then make sliding button knots on each end (see page 24).

Opposite
Necklaces tied with double button knots (from left to right):
African green powder glass beads; antique African head
pendant; the finished project necklace; amber pendant;
and Tibetan carnelian beads.

Double button knot necklace

This necklace, tied with a single length of cord, has double, single and sliding button knots interspersed with unpolished amethyst beads. Prepare the cord ends with sticky tape or PVA glue (see page 17) to help thread the cord back through the knot.

You will need

300cm (118in) 2mm satin cord
Seven unpolished amethyst beads

1. Anchor a bead at the middle of the cord, then, referring to pages 22–23, tie a loose knot and move it up close to the bead.

2. Start to weave the cord back through the knot, following the lead of the original cord . . .

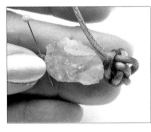

3. . . . pull the new cord through the loop, keeping it uncrossed by the side of the original cord . . .

4. . . . rotate the knot, then take the cord end through the next loop.

5. Continue rotating the knot, passing the cord under five single loops, then three double loops to finish the knot.

6. Make a second double button knot on the other side of the bead.

7. Make another double button knot and move it to leave a short length of cord between it and its neighbour. Thread on a bead, then make another double button knot.

8. Work the remaining lengths of the necklace with single button knots either side of a bead. Equalise the lengths of cord, then finish with sliding button knots (see page 24).

Opposite
Necklaces and earrings made with double button knots tied with one cord end (from left to right): necklace with dark blue Venetian glass lamp beads; earrings with handmade red glass beads; necklace with maroon horn beads and Greek ceramic round beads; the finished project necklace; and a matching pair of amethyst earrings.

Three-colour button knot bracelet

The button knots on this bracelet are all single button knots tied with one end of a cord around two different coloured cords.

You will need

150cm (59in) 2mm satin cord* of each colour

Bar and ring toggle fastener

* For a two-colour bracelet use 180cm (71in) of cord for each colour.

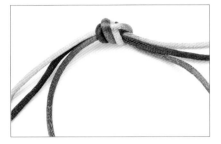

1. Tie a simple overhand knot with all three cords, 7.5cm (3in) from one end.

2. Referring to page 24, use the yellow cord to make a single button knot round the other cords.

3. Move the knot up against the overhand knot, then use the red cord to make a knot round the yellow and brown cords.

4. Move the red knot up against the yellow one, then make a brown knot round the red and yellow cords.

5. Move the brown knot up against the red one, then repeat steps 2–4 to continue the sequence of knots. When the bracelet is long enough, pass two cord ends through the ring half of the fastener.

6. Thread the end of one cord in a large-eyed tapestry needle, then pass it back through three knots.

7. Repeat step 6 with the other cord, but, this time take it back through just two knots.

8. Trim all three cords to leave just 2–3mm (1/8in), then seal the ends with a flame. Repeat steps 5–8 at the other end of the bracelet with the toggle half of the fastener.

The finished project bracelet, together with similar bracelets in other colourways. Some of these are tied with three cords, others with just two.

FLAT BUTTON KNOT

This variation of the button knot is tied with one end of a cord, which allows a series of knots to be tied side by side. A single flat button knot at one end of a necklace can be inserted through a large loop at the other end to form the closure (see pages 41–42). The finished knot, especially when worked with silky cords, may need a stitch or two on the back to stop it from twisting or loosening.

Flat button knot

Tying the knot

This knot can be tied in the hand, but I suggest you practise tying it on a cork mat. If you want to tie the knot with two cords, side by side, as shown opposite a cork mat is essential. In the diagrams below, previous knots would be on cord A.

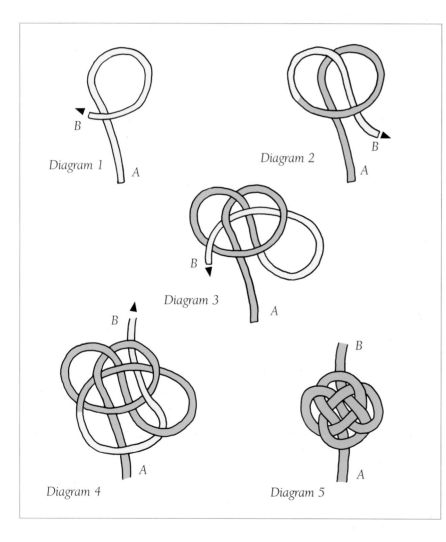

Diagram 1

Diagram 2

Diagram 3

Diagram 4

Diagram 5

1. Anchor cord A, then form a loop with cord B (diagram 1).

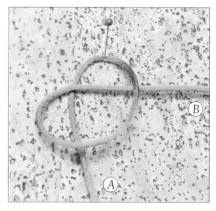

2. Take cord B round and down through the loop (diagram 2).

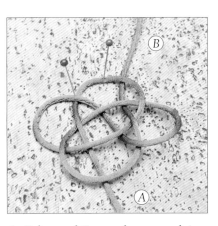

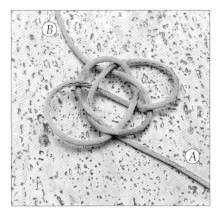

3. Form a loop, then weave cord B under, over, under and over the knotting (diagram 3).

4. Take cord B round over cord A, then weave it under, over, under and under the knotting (diagram 4).

5. Start to close the knot by pulling both ends of the cord.

6. Remove the knot from the pin board, then pull the cord through the knot to equalise the loops. At this point, if you wish, you can move the knot along the cord.

7. Continue adjusting the size of the loops until you are happy with the shape of the knot.

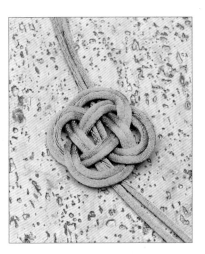

Tying the knot with two cords

The flat button knot can also look very good when tied with two cords. You can follow the step-by-step sequence, working with both cords at once, or you can work the knot with a single cord up to step 4, then weave the second cord through the knotting. Which ever way you choose to work, ensure that the cords are not allowed to twist over each other. They must sit flat and side by side throughout the knot.

CROSS KNOT

In Chinese a cross simply means ten. This knot gives a nice round loop and is very stable. It can also look very attractive as a sequence of knots tied with two different colours.

Tying the knot

This knot is best tied on a cork mat, with pins holding the shape of the loops. In the diagrams below, the knot is tied using two cord ends, A and B, but it can also be tied with just one cord end by starting at point D in diagram 3.

Front and back views of a cross knot.

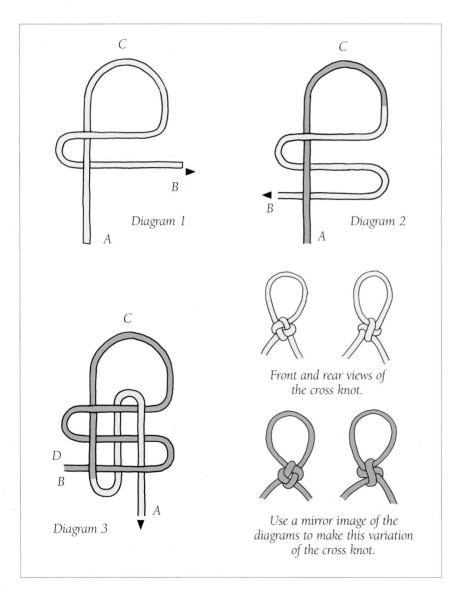

Diagram 1

Diagram 2

Diagram 3

Front and rear views of the cross knot.

Use a mirror image of the diagrams to make this variation of the cross knot.

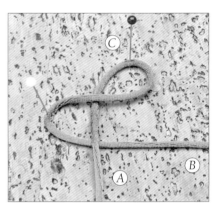

1. Anchor the middle of the cord at point C, and cord A at the bottom of the pin board. Form a U-bend with cord B taking it over then back under cord A (diagram 1).

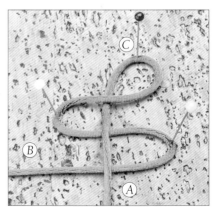

2. Form another U-bend, anchor this with a pin, then take cord B under cord A (diagram 2).

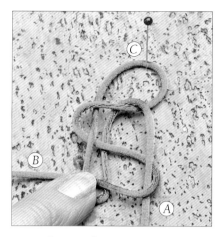

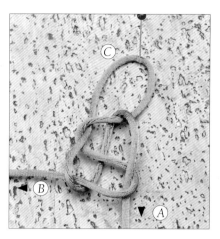

3. Anchor cord B, then take cord A up under the two U-bends in cord B, then back down, over two cords and under the third (diagram 3).

4. Start to close the knot by pulling cords A and B gently in the directions indicated.

5. Before fully tightening the knot, adjust the size of the top loop (or the position of the knot relative to previous ones) by pulling cord A and then cord B through the knot.

Cross knot necklace with a flat button knot fastener

This attractive necklace consists of a series of cross knots with beads threaded between each knot and is tied with leather cord. Use pairs of pins to secure each loop of the knot to the cork mat – single pins through the leather could leave unsightly marks.

The fastener is a flat button knot, also worked on the cork mat, which engages the first loop of the necklace.

You will need

2m (79in), 1.5mm (¹/₁₆in) diameter leather cord

Twelve rectangular tube beads

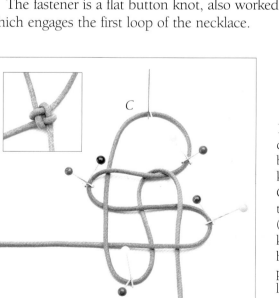

1. Referring to the diagrams opposite, build up an open cross knot on a cork mat. Carefully pull the knot tight, leaving a 3cm (1¼in) loop above the knot. You may find it helpful to reposition the pins that anchor each loop as the knot is pulled tighter.

Tightening tip

Keep the centre of the knot pattern flat as you tighten the knot, or you could lose its shape.

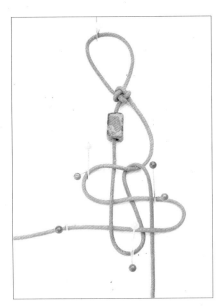

2. Thread a bead on the left-hand cord, then repeat step 1 to make another cross knot.

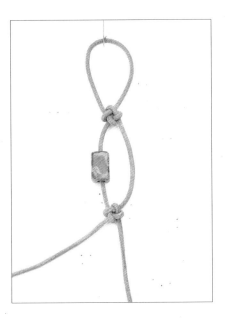

3. Pull this knot tight, leaving 3cm (1¼in) lengths of cord between it and the first knot. Repeat steps 1–3, keeping the loops between the knots evenly spaced, until the necklace is 43cm (17½in) long.

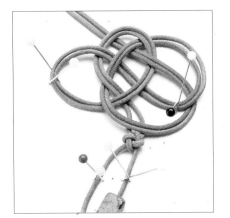

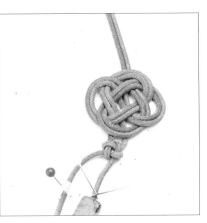

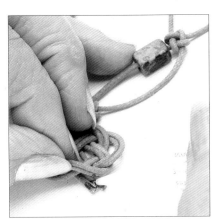

4. Referring to the diagrams on page 38, build up a double flat knot at the end of the necklace. Work on the cork mat and use pairs of pins to hold the cords flat.

5. Keeping both cords side by side, carefully pull the knot closed, tight up against the final cross knot.

6. Trim off the excess ends of the cords, then use instant glue to stick the trimmed ends to the underside of the knot.

7. Finally, using touches of instant glue, secure the beads in the middle of the loops.

Opposite
Bracelets and necklaces made with cross knots (from left to right).
Bracelet made using four cords. The cross knots were tied first with the outside pairs of cords then with the middle two cords. The cord ends were unravelled to make the tassel.
Bracelet with blue and green beads threaded along the cord between the cross knots.
The finished project necklace.
Dark brown leather necklace, again with a flat button knot and loop fastening.

DOUBLE COIN KNOT

This is a well known knot which, in the West, is referred to as the Josephine knot. To the Chinese the shape represents two overlapping antique coins and denotes great prosperity and long life. It is often hung over the entrances to shops and businesses to attract lots of customers and hence a good income.

A series of these knots tied side by side with one end of a firm cord looks lovely. The introduction of a second, different coloured cord can be very attractive. A variation of the knot, tied with both ends of the cord gives a series of knots one above another. The knot can also be used to join to cords (see page 46).

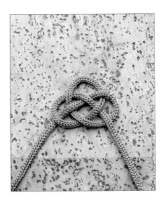

Double coin knot

Tying the knot with one end of a cord

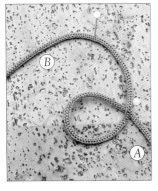

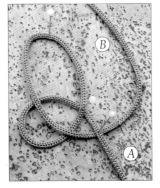

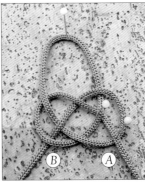

1. Anchor the right-hand cord at A and form a loop with cord end B. Use pins to hold the shape.

2. Form a second loop by taking cord B down over the first loop, then under the right-hand cord.

3. Complete the knot pattern by weaving cord B down through the two loops as shown.

4. Remove the pins and gently pull the knot into its final shape.

Tying the knot with two ends of a cord

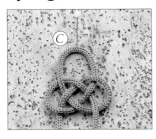

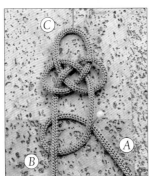

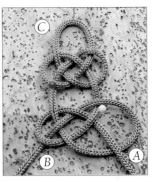

1. Anchor the centre of the cord at point C, then use both cord ends to tie a knot as shown above.

2. Form a loop with the right-hand cord A.

3. Take cord B round under cord A, then weave it down through the two loops as shown.

4. Gently pull the knot into shape.

44

Double coin knot necklace

Double coin knots are not very stable when tied with soft cord so I used firm braided cord for this project. Pay particular attention to the spacing and tightening of the knots; they should be equally spaced and all the same size. The necklace has a hook and eye fastener.

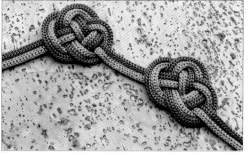

You will need

*Two 300cm (118in) lengths
of 2mm braided cord in
different colours*
Two flat leather crimps
Two split rings
Hook and eye fastener

*Leather crimp, split ring
and the hook part of the fastener.*

1. Referring to the step-by-step photographs opposite, anchor the right-hand end of the pair of cords and build up a double coin knot keeping the cords side by side.

2. Release the pin in the top loop, then tighten the knot by closing the loops as shown.

3. Working with the left-hand ends of the cords, build up a second knot. Tighten this knot to leave a short length of cords between it and the first knot.

4. Continue making knots until the necklace is long enough, then place the leather crimp on one end of the bracelet. Use a pair of pliers to clamp first one side then the other of the leather crimp.

5. Trim off the excess cords, then flame seal the exposed ends.

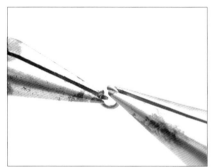

6. Use two pairs of pointed pliers to twist the ends of the split ring apart.

7. Secure the hook fastener to the leather crimp with the split ring. Repeat steps 4–7 to finish the other end of the necklace.

This variation of the double coin knot can be used to join two lengths of cord.

Opposite
The finished project necklace and a matching necklace and bracelet set. The double coin knots used for this set were tied with two ends of two cords.

DOUBLE CONNECTION KNOT

This is a very stable knot and looks especially good when it is tied with two different coloured cords.

Double connection knot

Tying the knot

1. Tie an overhand knot with the brown cord to form a loop enclosing the black cord.

2. Tie an overhand knot with the black cord to form a loop within the brown loop.

3. Arrange the two loops as shown.

4. Close the knot by pulling both cords at each end.

PROSPERITY KNOT

This knot takes its name from the fact that it has the appearance of a large number of double coin knots woven together. It looks best with a second cord of a different colour added after the tying of the first cord is complete. Although it can be used on its own, it does look good with a pendant attached. In this case, the pendant must be threaded on the cord before the knot is tied.

Prosperity knot tied with two colours

Tying the knot

Allow 40cm (16in) of cord for the knot itself, plus enough for the rest of the necklace. Practise tying the knot with a 1m (1yd) length of cord. I find the simplest way to tie this knot is to prepare a cork mat with seven pins arranged as shown; the columns are approximately 7cm (2¾in) apart and the rows 3cm (1½in) apart.

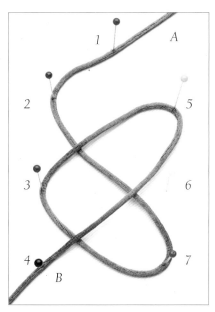

1. Anchor the middle of the cord at point 1, form an S-shape with cord end B and anchor this at points 2, 7 and 3. Take the cord back over itself and anchor it to points 5 and 4.

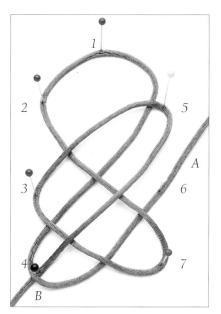

2. Pass the cord end A under the existing lay of the cord down to point 4. Take it over the cord at this point, then back up, under the existing lay of the cord, to point 6.

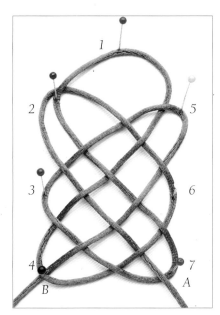

3. Now weave the end of the cord A over and under the existing lay of the cord, up and round point 2 then back down to point 7.

4. Check all the under and overs, then remove the pins and pull the knot to the required size.

Prosperity knot and double connection knot necklace

Black and rust-brown are the perfect match for the amber pendant of this lovely necklace. The shape of the pendant and the prosperity knot are balanced by the delicate shape of the double connection knots used to form the sides of the necklace. Double sliding button knots are used to close the necklace and make the length adjustable.

You will need

150cm (60in) length each of black and rust-brown 2mm satin cord

Amber pendant with a loop at the top

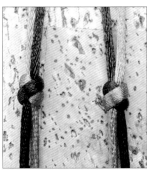

1. Centre the pendant on both cords and pin the middle of the cords to point 1. Referring to the instructions on page 49, weave an open knot. Keep the knotting flat with the cords side by side.

2. Remove the pins and gently pull the knot tight.

3. Referring to the instructions on page 48, make double connection knots with each pair of cords. Note that the left-hand knot has the black cord on top and the right-hand one the brown cord on top. Move the knots to leave 8cm (3¼in) between them and the prosperity knot.

4. Make a second set of double connection knots, 8cm (3¼in) away from the first set, then a third set another 8cm (3¼in) along the cord. Equalise the lengths of cord, then, referring to pages 24 and 32, make a double sliding button knot on each end. Trim off excess cord and seal the ends with a flame.

Opposite
The finished project necklace and a bracelet with wooden beads set between prosperity knots.

CLOVER LEAF KNOT

This knot is tied with one end of a cord, which makes it very versatile. The knot consists of inner U-bends and outer 'leaf' loops and is best tied on a cork mat. The number of loops can be varied from two up to five or six. For this reason, the knot is also known as a Flower knot. It is very attractive and is often used as the basis of more complicated Chinese combination knots. A four-leaved clover, for example, is considered to be very lucky by the Chinese. The knot is not very stable, especially when tied with a silky cord, so the body of the knot should be secured with a few stitches on the back.

Clover leaf knot

Tying the knot

The sequence of diagrams below show how to tie a knot with four U-bends and three leaf loops, but I have also included the final stage diagram for both two- and four-leaf knots.

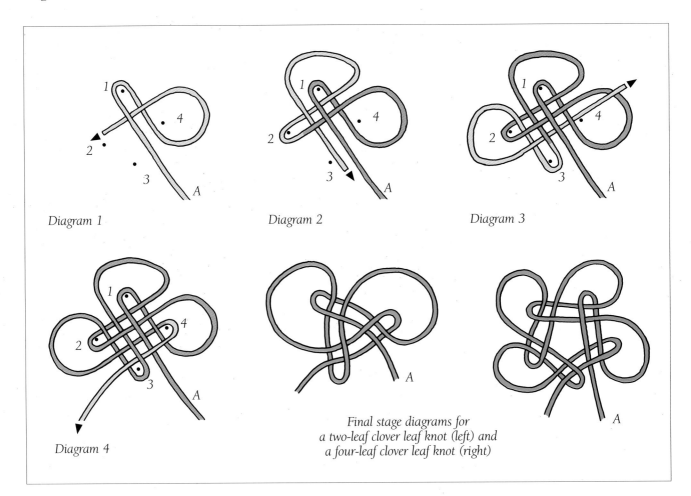

Diagram 1

Diagram 2

Diagram 3

Diagram 4

Final stage diagrams for a two-leaf clover leaf knot (left) and a four-leaf clover leaf knot (right)

Clover leaf knot necklace

This necklace is approximately 96cm (38in) long and incorporates two, three-loop cloverleaf knots and a series of button knots.

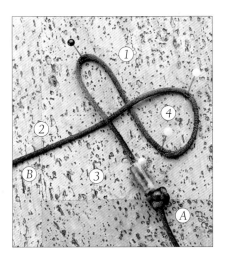

1. Referring to pages 22–23, make a single button knot, 40cm (16in) from one end of the cord, and thread a bead on the short end. Anchor cord end A, then use cord end B to make a U-bend round point 1 and a leaf loop round point 4. Take the cord over and under the U-bend and across to point 2 (diagram 1).

You will need

300cm (118in) length of 2mm satin cord

Five tubular ceramic beads

One round ceramic bead

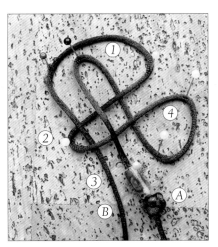

2. Make U-bend round point 2, take the cord under and over U-bend 1, and form a leaf loop round point 1. Take the cord over and under the U-bend 2 and across to point 3 (diagram 2).

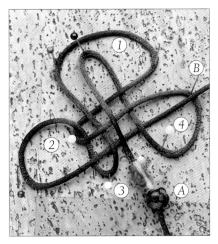

3. Repeat step 2 to make a U-bend round point 3 and a leaf loop round point 2. Take the cord over and under U-bend 3 and under both cords of U-bend 1 (diagram 3).

4. Make a U-bend round point 4, take the cord over both cords of U-bend 1, then under and over the cords of U-bend 3 (diagram 4).

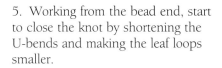

5. Working from the bead end, start to close the knot by shortening the U-bends and making the leaf loops smaller.

6. Continue pulling the cord through until the centre knot is tight and the leaf loops are the same size.

7. Take the short end of the cord back through the bead, trim off the excess cord and flame seal the end between the bead and button knot.

8. Make a second button knot and move it so that it is 2cm (¾in) away from the first. Make a third button knot and move this up against the second one. Add a tubular bead, then make two more button knots. Take the cord through a third tubular bead and the round bead, leave a 40cm (16in) long neck loop, then take the cord back through the round bead and the third tubular one. Repeat the design with two button knots, a tubular bead and a further two button knots.

9. Repeat steps 1–7 to finish the necklace with a button knot, tubular bead and cloverleaf knot on the other end of the cord.

Variation tip

If you insert a pair of sliding button knots in the neck loop, the necklace can be shortened to a fashionable choker length.

Opposite
The finished necklace and a matching brooch. I like asymmetrical designs, and this necklace would look just as good with one of the clover leaf knots pulled through the tubular bead to hang below the other. The brooch features a Pan Chang knot (see pages 60–61), with a sieve brooch-back sewn on the back, and two clover leaf knots tied below the bead.

GOOD LUCK KNOT

Chinese knots are considered to be tokens of love and affection. This Good Luck knot, like many of its fellow knots, should bring extra good fortune to the lucky wearer as well as to the giver of the knot.

Tying the knot

The diagrams below show how to tie this knot with three loops, but it can be tied with four or five loops. Theoretically even more loops are possible, but, in practice, the knotting would be almost impossible to control. A cork mat and pins are essential. The initial U-bends in the knotting should be approximately 12cm (5in) long.

Good Luck knot

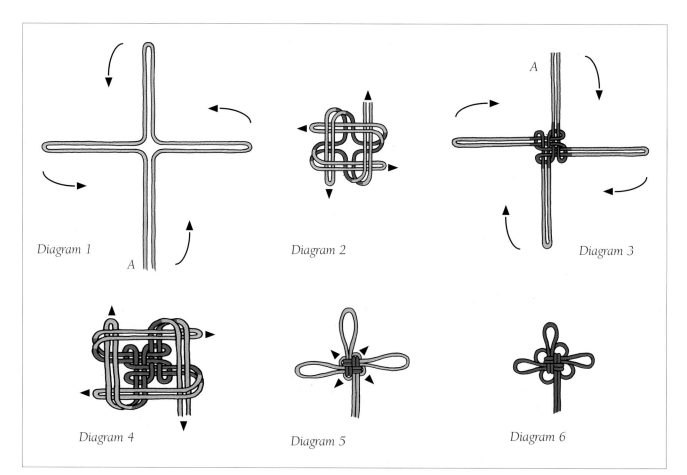

Diagram 1

Diagram 2

Diagram 3

Diagram 4

Diagram 5

Diagram 6

Good Luck knot pendant necklace

This necklace uses the Good Luck knot as a pendant. Its slightly asymmetrical shape adds to its charm and good looks. The loops are large and will keep their shape if you stiffen them with diluted PVA glue. The finished necklace (excluding the pendant) is 40cm (16in) long.

You will need

300cm (118in) length of 2mm satin cord

Sixteen assorted antiqued silver beads

Matching silver hook and eye fastener

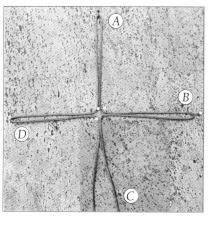

1. Fold the cord in half and pin the centre at point A. Arrange each end of the cord to form loops as shown.

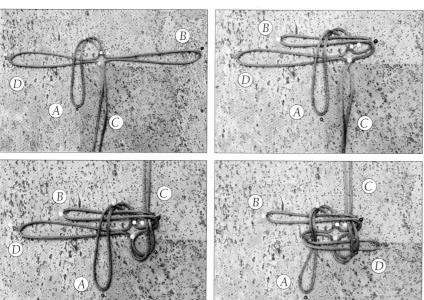

2. Fold loop A down over loop D. Fold loop B over and under the cords of loop A. Fold the cord ends C over and under the cords of loop B. Complete this step by folding loop D over and under the cords of loop C.

3. Pull the loops to close the knot.

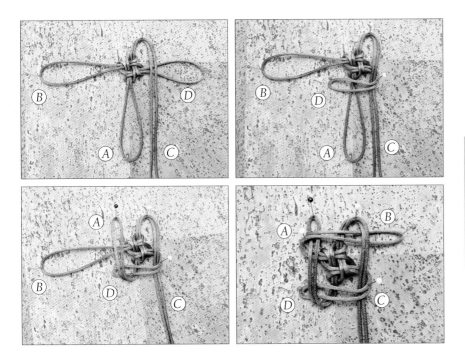

4. Now working in the opposite direction: fold cord ends C down over loop D; fold loop D over loop A; fold loop A over loop B; then complete this step by folding loop B over loop A and under loop C.

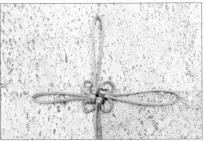

5. Pull the loops to close the knot, then pull out the small loops from the back of the knot. Adjust the large loops to size.

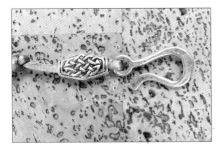

6. When you are happy with the shape, stiffen the back of the knot with some diluted PVA glue. Ten parts water to one part glue will stiffen the cord without affecting the colour of the cord too much.

7. Referring to page 28, use two cord ends to make a single button knot. Move this knot to leave a 1cm (½in) length of cord between it and the Good Luck knot. Working along each cord in turn, tie two groups of four single button knots separated by three beads with a short length of cord between each group. Leave a short gap, then work two single button knots separated by a bead.

8. Equalise the ends of the cords, thread each end through a bead, through the ring of the fastener and back through the bead. Trim off excess cord, add a touch of instant glue if necessary, then flame seal the ends to complete the necklace.

Opposite
The finished project necklace and a
similar necklace with matching earrings.

PAN CHANG KNOT

In Chinese, Pan Chang means endless. The endless pattern of this knot represents birth and death, and indicates that life can exist for ever – one of the most basic concepts of Chinese Buddhism. As one of the Eight Buddhist Treasures, it also represents the mysteries of the Universe and is also known as the Mystic Knot. As such it is considered to bring great good fortune to the wearer and beholder alike. As if this is not enough, the Chinese word for this knot shares the same sound as the word for happiness, so the knot is also taken to mean happiness without end.

Pan Chang knot

Tying the knot

The initial knotting is flat but, when the knot is tightened, the woven cords separate into the two layers, making it very stable. It looks difficult but, if you follow the overs and unders, it turns out very well. The secret is in the tightening and the outer loops must be even. Hold the square centre of the knot, and pull the outside loops equally in both directions at once, and as consistently even as possible.

A cork mat and pins are definitely required! Practise tying the knot with a 2m (2yd) length of cord. At first, try working with two different coloured cords, pinned together at point C so that, when you are tightening the knot, you can concentrate on one colour at a time.

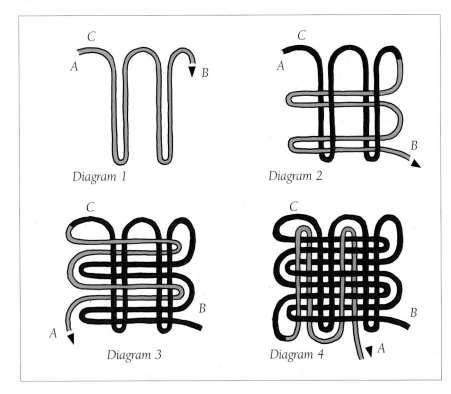

Diagram 1

Diagram 2

Diagram 3

Diagram 4

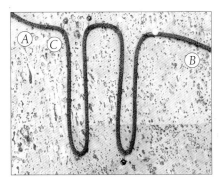

1. Secure the middle of the cord at point C and cord end A at the edge of the cork mat. Form two vertical loops with cord B (diagram 1) . . .

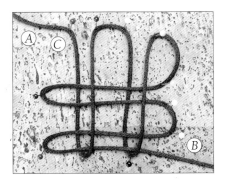

2. . . . then make two horizontal loops, taking each of these under, over, under and over the vertical lengths of cord (diagram 2).

60

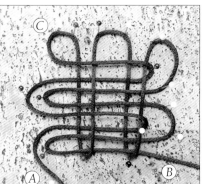

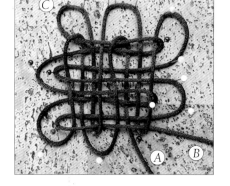

3. Now, using cord end A, lay in two further horizontal loops – work each of these loops by taking the cord over all four vertical cords, then back under them all (diagram 3).

4. Complete the knotting by weaving two further vertical loops. Check all the unders and overs are as shown in diagram 4.

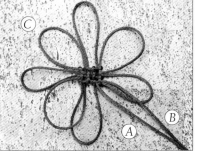

5. Close the knot by pulling on the outer seven loops. As the knot tightens, the cords that were sitting side by side, will move on top of each other.

6. Starting at point C, pull cord B through the knot to reduce the size of the loops 1–4. Now pull cord A through the knot to reduce the size of loops 5–7.

7. Repeat step 6 until all the loops are at the required size and the centre knot is neat and square. If the loops are left large, stiffen the knot with PVA glue (see page 58).

Pan Chang knot necklace

This is a Western style necklace with a Chinese flavour. A Pan Chang knot pendant is decorated with a few beads attached to a head pin. More beads and button knots make up the sides of the necklace, the length of which is made adjustable by two sliding button knots.

You will need

300cm (118in) length of 2mm satin cord

Seven round Venetian style glass lamp beads

Brass head pin

Two small beads with small holes

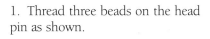

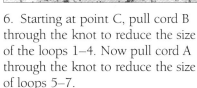

1. Thread three beads on the head pin as shown.

2. Use a pair of wire cutters to trim the head pin to leave 1.5cm (½in) above the bead.

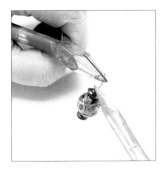

3. Use two pairs of pliers to form a ring on the end of the head pin.

4. Set the completed bead pendant in the middle of the cord.

5. Referring to page 28, use both cord ends to tie a single button knot.

6. Move the button knot tight up against the bead pendant so that it covers the ring.

7. Referring to the instructions on pages 60–61, anchor the button knot at point C and tie a Pan Chang knot. Pull it to size, then work a second button knot with the free ends of the cords.

8. Separate the cords, then, working on each length in turn, make two button knots with a bead between them. Move this group to leave a short length of cord between it and the pendant knots.

9. Now make a group of four button knots with a bead between and move this group to leave a short length of cord between it and the first group. Repeat this step to make another group of knots.

10. Equalise the lengths of cord, then, referring to page 24, make sliding button knots to complete the necklace.

Design observation

When it comes to original design, there are subtle differences between Eastern and Western ideas.

I like asymmetrical designs, and I often leave spaces between knots, but a Chinese friend told me that she did not feel comfortable with them.

She said that, traditionally, a Chinese person would not leave gaps between knots, and that symmetry is a very important aspect of Chinese design.

Opposite

The Pan Chang knot features in all these necklaces and earrings. Note that the loops have been pulled out in several different ways to illustrate how the shape of the knot can be altered. The button knots used along the length of the necklaces represent the worker bees, and the Pan Chang knot the queen bee of Chinese knots.

SNAKE KNOT

Snake knot

The snake is one of the twelve animals in the Chinese horoscope. It is regarded as a bringer of good fortune, and also the guardian of treasure. In China it is considered to be very unlucky to injure or kill a snake which comes into your house. Apparently there are not many poisonous varieties in China!

Tying the knot

This is a very snakelike knot when made up and can twist and turn just like its namesake. Two cord ends are required to tie the knot. It looks good when worked with two different colours, but you can practise the knot with a 2m (2yd) length of cord folded in the middle. This will make a 15cm (6in) snake. A cork mat is useful for the first few stages.

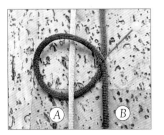

1. Make a loop with cord B, taking it under and over cord A.

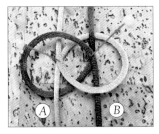

2. Now make a loop with cord A, taking it over and under the first loop and back under itself.

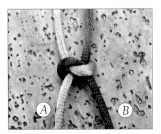

3. Gently pull both cords to close the knot.

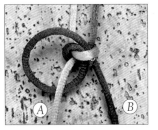

4. Take cord B under cord A and down through its loop as shown.

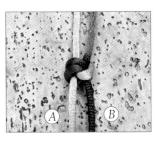

5. Gently pull cord B to close the knot. Note that the double closed loop on the left-hand side of this step only appears at the beginning of the snake.

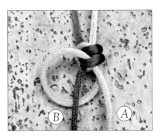

6. Turn the knotting over and take cord A under cord B and down through the lower of the two closed loops as shown.

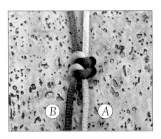

7. Gently pull cord A to close the knot.

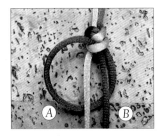

8. Turn the knotting over and repeat steps 4–7 until the snake is long enough.

When you are confident with the method of knotting and have settled into a rhythm, you will find it quicker to hold the knotting in your left hand and knot from left to right. Rotate the knotting towards you to turn it over after each knot.

Snake knot necklace

Snake knots are ideal for making a heavier than usual necklace. Here, a double coin knot, tied with two cords, supports the turquoise pendant. The central design is balanced with a button knot between two glass beads on each side. The sides are then worked with continuous snake knots. The finished necklace is approximately 44cm (17¼in) long.

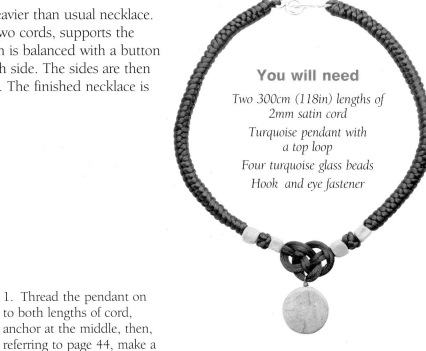

You will need

Two 300cm (118in) lengths of 2mm satin cord

Turquoise pendant with a top loop

Four turquoise glass beads

Hook and eye fastener

1. Thread the pendant on to both lengths of cord, anchor at the middle, then, referring to page 44, make a double coin knot.

2. Working on one side of the pendant at a time, thread both cords through a bead and make a single button knot. Move this knot up against the bead, then thread on another bead.

3. Referring to the instructions opposite make a series of snake knots until the knotting is 15cm (6in) long.

4. Attach the hook and ring fasteners to the ends in a similar manner to that described on page 36.

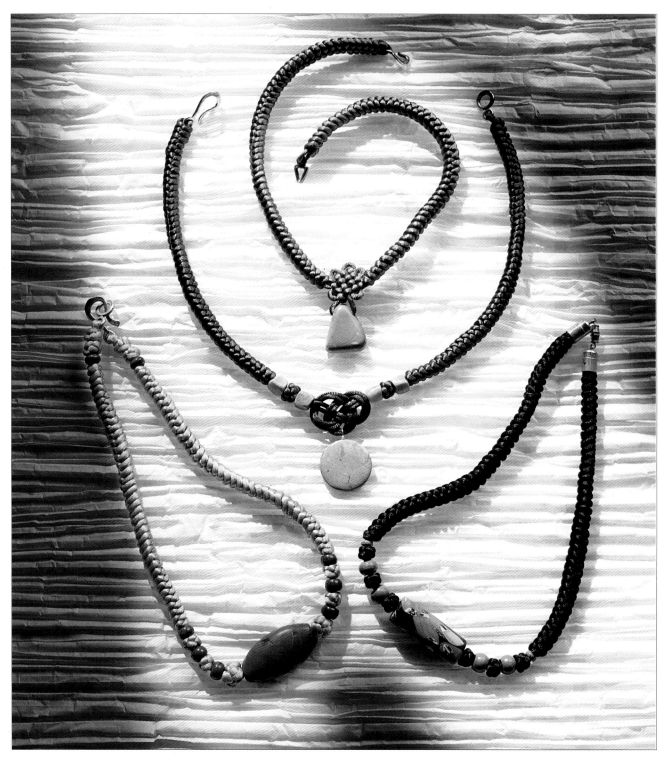

The finished project necklace and other variations, all of which
have snake knot sides. The necklace at bottom left has a
carnelian bead as the central feature, while a multicoloured
handmade glass bead adorns the one at bottom right.

Necklaces and earrings using round brocade knots (see overleaf). The left-hand necklace has a handmade, fused glass pendant connected to an enlarged loop of a round brocade knot. The sides of the necklace are decorated with coloured glass beads in matching colours interspersed with button knots. The other necklace is the project on page 69. The earrings have round brocade knots with very small loops and silver beads.

ROUND BROCADE KNOT

The round pattern of this knot denotes good fortune, as, to the Chinese, a circle represents the origin of all creation, and a ring is the symbol of eternity.

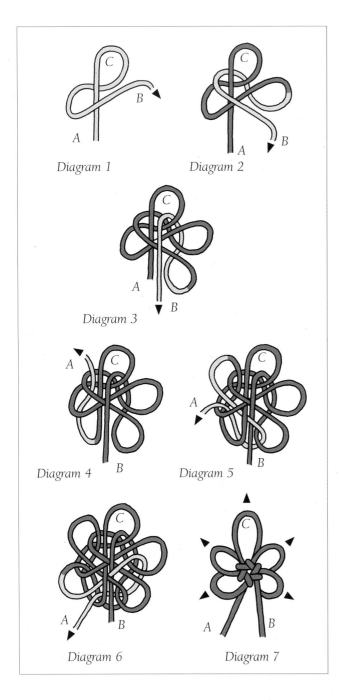

Diagram 1

Diagram 2

Diagram 3

Diagram 4

Diagram 5

Diagram 6

Diagram 7

Round brocade knot

Tying the knot

This knot is best tied on a cork mat. It is usually tied with two working cord ends, but, if you are very patient, it is possible to tie it with one working end. Try to keep all the loops roughly equal in size so that they remain so when the knot is closed.

Start by anchoring the middle of the cord at point C and cord A at the bottom of the cork board, then take cord B under and over cord A to form the first loops (diagram 1).

Continue making loops with cord B as shown in diagrams 2 and 3, then anchor this cord.

Now, weave loops with cord A as shown in diagrams 4–6 to complete the knotting.

At this stage you can make the loops smaller by pulling the cord through from the beginning and following steps 2 to 6. Close the centre of the knot by pulling the loops as shown in diagram 7.

Round brocade knot necklace

A round brocade knot forms a pendant for this delicate necklace, the sides of which are decorated with button knots and a multitude of different coloured beads. A few small matching beads were attached to the bottom loop of the round brocade knot with a head pin. The finished necklace is approximately 41cm (17¼in) long.

You will need

250cm (98in) 1.5mm cord

Brass head pin

Two small brass beads

Sixty six small beads
in assorted colours

Brass hook and loop
fastener

1. Anchor the middle of the cord at point C, then, referring to the diagrams opposite, tie a round brocade knot.

2. Referring to pages 28–29, tie two button knots with a bead between them. Move this group up close to the round brocade knot.

3. Separate the two cords, then, tie two button knots with eleven beads between them. Move this group to leave a short gap between it and the pendant knots.

4. Now work a group of two button knots and three beads. Move these to leave a gap between it and the previous group.

5. Repeat steps 3 (once) and 4 (twice), equalising the length of each side of the necklace. Take the cord end through the ring of the fastener and back through the last group of button knots and beads. Trim off the excess cord and seal the end.

6. Finally, referring to pages 61–62, thread some beads on a head pin then use two pairs of pliers to form a ring through the loop of the round brocade knot. Stiffen the loops of the knot with diluted PVA glue (see page 58).

VIRTUE KNOT

This knot has a pattern similar to an ancient Buddhist motif that symbolises the sun, fire, the Buddha's heart, complete virtue, and power over evil. It is the sign for ten thousand, Wan Tzu, and is said to come from heaven, and stands for the accumulation of good fortune.

Virtue knot

Tying the knot

This knot is not very stable and needs a stitch or two to keep it in shape, especially when worked with silky cord. It lends itself very well to the addition of beads on the loops.

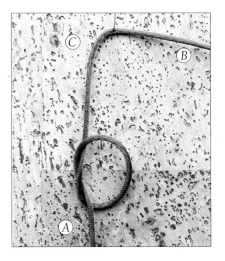

1. Anchor the middle of the cord at point C, then make an overhand knot with cord end A.

2. Make an overhand knot with cord B, taking the cord through the loop in cord A.

> **Tying variation**
> *If the cords are pulled tight after step 2, a knot without side loops results. This is known as a True Lover's knot.*

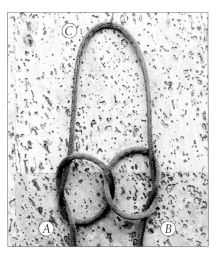

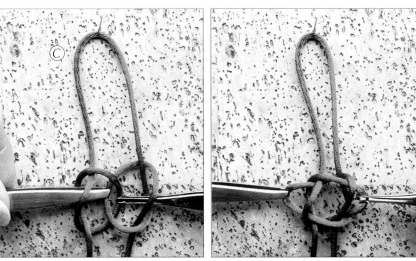

3. Pull the two loops through the overhand knots. Tweezers have been used to show the movement, but it would be better to use your fingers.

4. Continue pulling the loops to tighten the knot.

Virtue knot bracelet

A series of virtue knots, the loops of which are threaded with antique green glass beads, creates this beautiful bracelet which will glow on your wrist. The last beaded knot and the initial loop form the closure. The finished bracelet is 24cm (9½in) long.

You will need

200cm (79in) 2mm satin cord
Nine large green glass beads
Sixty small blue, turquoise and green glass beads

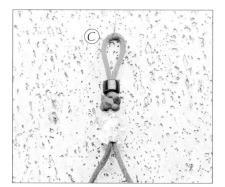

1. Anchor the middle of the cord at point C, thread on a small blue bead, then, referring to pages 28–29, use both cord ends make a single button knot, Move the knot up against the bead, leaving a 2cm (¾in) closure loop. Referring to page 42, secure the blue bead with instant glue. Thread both cord through one of the large green beads.

2. Thread three small beads on to each length of cord, then, referring to the diagram opposite, tie two entwined overhand knots; arrange the beads as shown.

3. Pull the loops and beads through the overhand knots.

4. Pull the ends of the cords to close the knot. Pull the cords through the knot to adjust the size of the loops and position the knot tight up against the glass bead.

5. Repeat steps 2–4 until the bracelet is 24m (9½in) long.

6. When the last virtue knot has been tightened, add a final small bead, trim off the excess cord and flame seal the end to secure the bead and finish the bracelet. The last virtue knot acts as the fastener.

The finished project bracelet together with a similar design that has single beads on the side loops of the virtue knot.

*Two necklaces tied with flat knots. The bottom one, tied with two lengths of
green and two lengths of blue cord, is the project described on pages 74–75.
In the top necklace, which is tied with three colours of cord, the green cord that
appears in the centre double coin knot forms the lazy cords of the two sides.*

FLAT KNOT

This knot will be familiar to readers as the Western Square Knot, or Reef Knot. The Ancient Egyptians and Greeks called it the Hercules Knot, so it has a long and varied history. It is a very popular knot for necklace and bracelet making. It is more versatile to have a pair of cords in the centre, known as 'lazy' cords.

Flat knot

Tying the knot

The flat knot consists of two overhand knots: the first is worked left over right, around the lazy cords; and the second is worked right over left, also around the lazy cords.

Variation tip

If in step 2 you repeat step 1 (a left over right followed by another left over right) the series of knots will twist into a spiral. This form has the popular name of Granny Knot.

1. Tie an overhand knot, taking the green cord over the lazy cords and the yellow cord under them.

2. Now tie a second overhand knot, again taking the green cord over the lazy cords and the yellow one under them.

Flat knot choker

The centre of this necklace has a double coin knot, tied with two lengths of blue cord and two lengths of green. The outer two cords of the four on each side of the necklace are used to tie a series of flat knots about the middle two cords. The necklace is closed with a hook and eye fastener.

3. Pull the flat knot tight, then repeat steps 1 and 2.

4. Repeat step 3 until the knotting is long enough. The green cord must always be on top of the lazy cords, and the yellow one under them.

You will need

100cm (39in) each of 2mm blue and green braided cord

250cm (98in) each of 2mm blue and green braided cord

Two flat leather crimps

Hook and eye fastener

1. Referring to page 46, tie a double coin knot. Arrange for the short length of each colour to form the lazy centre cords of the flat knots.

2. Now, working on the green side of the necklace and referring to the instructions opposite, tie the first two overhand knots.

3. Tighten the knot, pulling the cords through until the knot is tight up against the double coin knot.

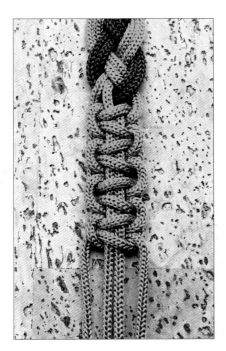

4. Continue tying pairs of overhand knots and tightening them against each other. Keep the tension and knot size the same along the whole length of the necklace.

5. When the necklace is long enough, use one of the outer two cords to make a single button knot around the other three cords (see pages 24 and 36). Trim and flame seal the working ends. Referring to page 46, secure the leather crimp to the lazy cords, trim and flame seal these, then use the split ring to add the fastener. Repeat steps 2–5 with the blue cords to complete the other side of the necklace.

PLAFOND KNOT

Plafond is the French word for ceiling, and this knot is similar to the design in the centre of the ceilings in Chinese temples and palaces. It is also known as the Well knot.

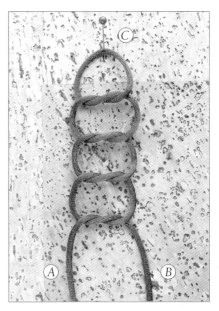

Plafond knot

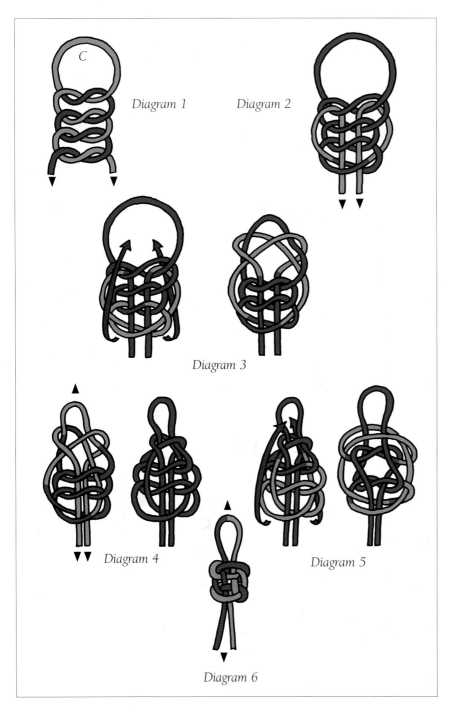

Diagram 1

Diagram 2

Diagram 3

Diagram 4

Diagram 5

Diagram 6

Tying the knot

This is a very satisfying knot to tie. It has an attractive pattern, is very stable and looks good with beads or a pendant added to it. It is tied with two working cord ends. At first glance, it looks rather daunting! However, when you have mastered it once or twice, it is easy to do, and this method is easy to remember. If you reverse the overhand knots in diagram 1 (to right over left), the design will be reversed.

1. Anchor the middle of the cord, then tie four (left over right) overhand knots (diagram 1).

2. Take cord A up to the top of the knotting, over the left-hand side of the top loop and down through the overhand knots. Take the cord B up to the top of the knotting, under the right-hand side of the top loop and down through the overhand knots (diagram 2).

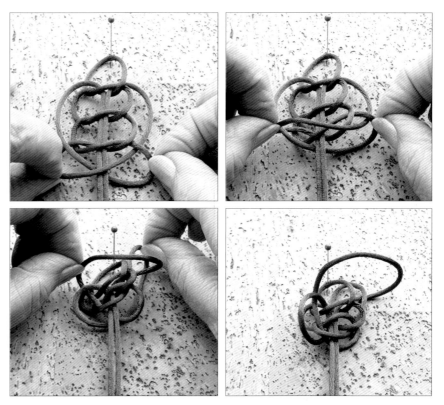

3. Following this sequence of photographs, take the bottom two loops to the top of the knotting – the left-hand one up over the knotting and the right-hand one up under it (diagram 3).

4. Straighten out the loops to flatten the knot and pull the cords through the knotting to lose any large loops (diagram 4).

5. Repeat steps 3 and 4 with the new bottom loops (diagram 5) to complete the knotting.

6. Pull the knot closed, then adjust its size by pulling the cord through the knotting (diagram 6).

Plafond knot necklace

The beautiful, handmade fused-glass pendant used for this necklace is complemented by the dark blue satin cord, the neat square plafond knot and the beads and button knots on the sides. A perfect combination! The sliding button knot finish makes it into a variable length necklace, the maximum length of which is 76cm (30in).

You will need

400cm (160in) 2mm satin cord
Glass pendant with a channel for the cord to pass through
Six glass beads in matching colours

1. Thread the pendant on to the middle of the cord, then tie a plafond knot with the two ends of cord.

2. Working along each length of cord tie two groups of six button knots with a bead in the middle. Move these groups to leave 3cm (1¼in) lengths of cord between the plafond knot and the start of the first group and the end of this group and the start of the second.

3. Leave a 4cm (1½in) length of cord then tie two more button knots with a bead between them.

4. Equalise the length of cord on each side of the necklace, then tie a sliding button knot on each end.

Opposite
The finished project necklace together with a necklace featuring a lapis bead pendant below a plafond knot. This necklace is also finished with button knots and beads. The earrings are each tied with a plafond knot and a button knot separated by a silver bead. Each earring is decorated with a silver disc from which tiny beads and silver pendants are suspended on seven silver wires.

INDEX